All About Me
Spanish Write & Read Books

15 Fun-Shaped Book Patterns
With Motivating Prompts to Get Kids Excited About Writing!

by Alyse Sweeney

S C H O L A S T I C
PROFESSIONAL BOOKS

New York • Toronto • London • Auckland • Sydney
Mexico City • New Delhi • Hong Kong • Buenos Aires

Cover design by Norma Ortiz
Cover and interior illustrations by Rusty Fletcher
Interior design by Victoria Worthington
Translated by Susana Pasternac
ISBN: 0-439-49870-8
Copyright © 2003 by Alyse Sweeney.
All rights reserved. Printed in the U.S.A.

2 3 4 5 6 7 8 9 10   40   09 08 07 06 05 04 03

Contents

Introduction..4

How to Use This Book...5

Follow-up Activities 6

All About Me Spanish Write & Read Books

Un libro sobre mí 9

Mi primera semana en la escuela.................................13

Te presento a mi familia 17

Te presento a mi amigo/a, _____ 21

¡Es Halloween!..24

¡Feliz Día de Acción de Gracias!................................28

Fiestas de invierno 31

El libro de mi cumpleaños 35

¡Es hora de comer!..39

Mis ojos 43

Mi animal favorito..47

Nuestra excursión 51

¿Qué tiempo hace?...55

¡Vivan los libros!..59

Cuando sea grande...62

Introduction

Watch your young writers blossom with *All About Me Spanish Write & Read Books*! Kids flourish as writers when given the opportunity to write about topics that they know and care about. These fifteen reproducible books guide children as they write about themselves and their immediate world. You'll find that the books are easily integrated into your curriculum with topics such as school, family, friends, favorite animals, holidays, weather, and more.

The fun-shaped book patterns make the writing process lively and appealing to kids. With guidance, children can cut out the patterns and assemble the books by themselves. They'll also enjoy personalizing their books by adding illustrations and coloring the covers. Once finished, the books make an easy and beautiful wall display inviting others to read all about your students!

All About Me Spanish Write & Read Books will engage all of your beginning writers. The books can be used in a variety of ways, depending upon the literacy development of your students. Younger children can complete one page each day, binding the pages together at the end of the week. Younger children will also benefit from the picture icons to guide them in their reading. Children are invited to circle the pictures and text that apply to them: foods they like, games they play, places they've visited, and so forth. More advanced learners will be able to write in greater detail and work more independently as they complete their books.

Encourage children to share their *All About Me Spanish Write & Read Books* at home. Children will gain valuable reading practice as they read their books to family members and friends. When kids share their writing with others, they gain confidence as writers. And as they gain confidence, they'll be motivated to write more and more! The books also provide parents with an important opportunity to observe and support their child's literacy development. Plus, sending the books home is a great way to open up discussion between children and their families about what they are doing in school.

All About Me Spanish Write & Read Books are a fun and easy way to foster confidence in your early readers and writers. They also provide a wonderful window into learning about your students as they share their own thoughts and experiences. Enjoy!

How to Use This Book

ASSEMBLING THE BOOKS
To assemble the books, copy a set of pages for each student on standard 8 1/2- by 11-inch paper. Cut out the pages around the book's shape. Arrange the pages in order and punch holes in the marked places. Tie string through the holes to bind the book pages together. Model the process for students so that they can assemble the books on their own.

PRE-WRITING WARM-UP
Set the stage for writing by discussing the book's topic with the class. This pre-writing discussion will help students activate prior knowledge. After this initial introduction, it is helpful to "walk through" each book with students before they begin writing. Read the prompts on each page so that students understand what they will be writing about. You may wish to complete a sample book and share it with students before they begin writing.

TIME TO WRITE
Explain to children that, like journals, *All About Me Spanish Write & Read Books* are a place for children to write down their own experiences, feelings, and opinions. Let children know that these books will allow them to share aspects of themselves with their classmates, teacher, and families. Explain that they will be able to personalize the books with their own writing and illustrations. Have children decorate their book covers when they have finished writing.

SHARE THE JOURNAL
Children will experience many benefits when they read their books to classmates, families, and friends. By sharing their books, children will view themselves as writers. Children will also develop reading skills and build fluency when they read their journals to others. And because *All About Me Spanish Write & Read Books* capture the thoughts, experiences, and interests of the writer, they also provide a tremendous opportunity for students to get to know one another. Children will realize that there are things they share in common with others, and that there are things that make every individual unique.

FOLLOW-UP ACTIVITIES
After students complete and share their books, you and your students may wish to continue to explore the topic. On pages 6–8, you'll find suggestions and activities for extending each book topic further. These follow-up activities include suggestions for related reading, writing, drawing, role-playing, discussion, and more.

Follow-up Activities

UN LIBRO SOBRE MÍ

Invite children to personalize their book cover by drawing their face and adding yarn for hair. Tally up the responses that children gave for their favorite animals, games, foods, and places. Draw a bar graph on chart paper for each category. Invite children to color in a square to show which is their favorite in each category. Show students how to read the graph and ask them to determine the most popular item in each category.

MI PRIMERA SEMANA EN LA ESCUELA

To encourage positive feelings and a sense of accomplishment after the first week of school, brainstorm a list of things your students have learned so far in your classroom. Be specific as you generate a list of what they have learned. Here are some suggestions:
- songs and games
- books and poems
- safety and class rules

TE PRESENTO A MI FAMILIA

Discuss ways that your students' families might differ. On chart paper, list similarities and differences. You might ask children about languages, foods, entertainment, and so on.

TE PRESENTO A MI AMIGO, _____

This book provides a good opportunity to lead a discussion about how students think they should treat their friends, and how they like their friends to treat them. This is also a good opportunity to talk about ways to make new friends. Invite students to think of ways to make new friends and role-play situations in which they are meeting people for the first time.

¡ES HALLOWEEN!

Make a graph of students' favorite Halloween candy. On a bar graph, write the names of several kinds of candy (or glue a wrapper from each kind) along the bottom of the graph. Write the numbers 1–12 along the left side of the graph. Read aloud the types of candy and have students draw an X in a box to show their favorite kind. Help students read the graph to find out which is the most popular candy.

¡FELIZ DÍA DE ACCIÓN DE GRACIAS!

Use the children's responses in their books to make a class list of what they are thankful for. What else can they add to the list? Invite students to illustrate their ideas on a mural entitled "Damos Gracias." Display children's Thanksgiving books around the mural as a frame.

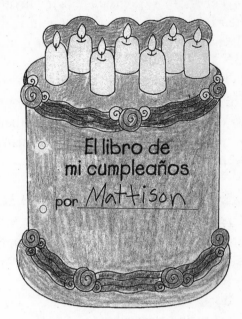

FIESTAS DE INVIERNO

Encourage students to present information about the holidays that they celebrate. Ask students to bring in something that relates to the holiday they are going to talk about. After students have shared information with the class, invite them to make cards for one another that reflect what they have learned about the various holidays. Children can also make holiday cards for other friends and their family members.

Teaching Tip: For children who celebrate more than one winter holiday, make an extra copy of pages 33 and 34. Encourage children to write and draw about all of the holidays they celebrate.

EL LIBRO DE MI CUMPLEAÑOS

Make a birthday timeline by hanging labels for the twelve months on a bulletin board or wall. Have children draw pictures of themselves and write their name and birthday on their drawing. Ask children to take turns attaching their paper in the correct spot on the birthday timeline. Keep the birthday timeline displayed for reference throughout the year. When it is a child's birthday, attach a special birthday marker, such as a cake or party hat, to his or her drawing.

¡ES HORA DE COMER!

Have children create a menu of their favorite foods. Bring in menus from restaurants as models to show students. On chart paper, list the following categories: breakfast, snacks, lunch, dinner, dessert, and beverages. Brainstorm food items for each category. Then give students one large piece of construction paper each and ask them to fold it in half. On the front cover, have students make up a restaurant name that incorporates their own name. On the inside, they can list foods they would like their restaurant to serve for each meal of the day. Remind children to refer to the class list to help them with spelling, if necessary. Invite students to decorate their menus with illustrations or with pictures cut from magazines and catalogs.

MIS OJOS

Have children think about other parts of their body in the same way they thought about their eyes as they were writing. What are all the things they can do with their hands, feet, nose, mouth, and so on? Give each student a large sheet of craft paper. Have students work in pairs to trace each other on the paper. Invite students to write and draw on their outlines about things they can do with their legs, arms, hands, feet, and so on.

MI ANIMAL FAVORITO

Lead a guessing game using the information about students' favorite animals on page 2 of their books. Ask each student to share the information about the animal's features and size before the class guesses what the animal is.

For another extension activity, invite children to research their favorite animal. On page 3 of their books, children write something that they would like to know about their favorite animal. Have children research the answer to their question. Provide appropriate books and resources.

NUESTRA EXCURSIÓN

This is a great book to do as a follow-up to a class field trip. Use students' books to compile a list of what the children learned on the field trip. Send the list home to parents.

Have students work in pairs to plan a field trip that they would like to take. Ask them to think about questions such as:

- *Where would you like to go?*
- *How would we get there?*
- *Whom would we meet when we are there?*
- *What would we learn?*
- *What would we see?*
- *What sounds would we hear?*
- *What questions would you ask?*
- *What do you think you would learn on the field trip?*

¿QUÉ TIEMPO HACE?

Make pairs of weather cards for a game of weather concentration. Write the words *soleado, lluvioso, ventoso, nublado, helado,* and *nevado* on index cards. Draw or glue pictures depicting the weather words on the cards. Explain to students that they need to try to remember where the cards are in order to make matches.

For another extension activity, ask students to think about rainy day activities. As a class, brainstorm a list of activities that students like to do on rainy days. Ask students to share their responses from page 3 of their book about what they like to do when it rains. Encourage them to look around the classroom as they think about what other fun indoor activities they can add to the list. Display the list when it rains for kids to refer to for productive indoor activities.

¡VIVAN LOS LIBROS!

Have children write a book review about the book they featured in their Write & Read book. Create book review forms with some or all of the following information: title, author, setting, favorite character, what the book was about, and why the student liked the book.

CUANDO SEA GRANDE . . .

After students complete their books, have them work in pairs to interview each other about their future jobs. Ask students to imagine that they are grown up and that they are in the profession they wrote about on page 2 of their books. Have them think about what their day might be like as a grown-up in this job. Then invite pairs of students to "interview" each other. You may wish to brainstorm together a list of questions that children can ask their partners about their jobs. To extend this activity, invite children to interview a family member about his or her profession. Children can share what they learned with their classmates the next day.

Un libro sobre mí

por _____

Me llamo

_____.

Tengo _____ años de edad.

Mi animal favorito es _____.

Mi juego favorito es _____.

Mi comida favorita es _____.

○ Mi lugar favorito es _____.

Este es mi retrato.

○

1

All About Me Spanish Write & Read Books • Scholastic Professional Books •

Estos son algunos de los lugares que he visitado. (Encierra en un círculo el lugar que hayas visitado.)

biblioteca

parque

zoológico

playa

○
granja

montañas

También he visitado _____.

Me gustaría visitar _____.

○ Me gustaría visitar este lugar porque _____

_____

_____

_____

_____.

2

Acabo de aprender a

_____

_____

_____

_____.

En este dibujo estoy yo haciendo lo que
acabo de aprender.

Quiero aprender a _____

_____

_____.

3

All About Me Spanish Write & Read Books • Scholastic Professional Books •

Mi primera semana
en la escuela

por _____

Este año estoy en _____.

(tu grado)

Mi maestra/o se llama _____.

Este es el retrato de mi maestra/o.

Mi maestra/o me enseñó a _____

_____.

1

En mi primera semana en la escuela conocí a _____ personas.

Algunos de sus nombres son _____

_____

_____

_____

_____.

Me gusta conocer gente porque _____

_____

_____

_____

_____.

2

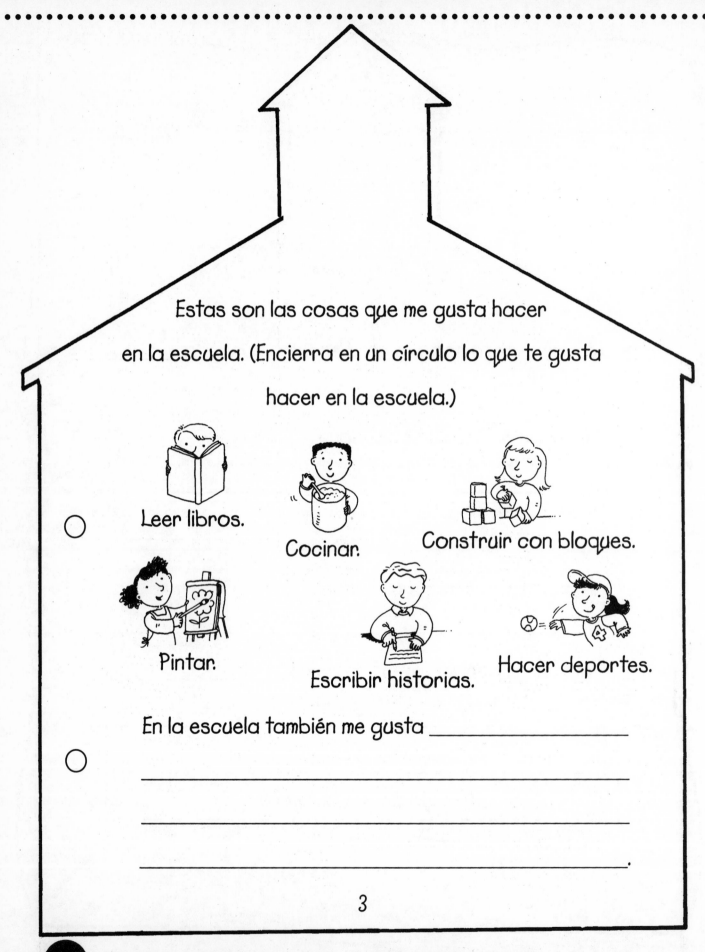

Estas son las cosas que me gusta hacer en la escuela. (Encierra en un círculo lo que te gusta hacer en la escuela.)

Leer libros.

Cocinar.

Construir con bloques.

Pintar.

Escribir historias.

Hacer deportes.

En la escuela también me gusta _____

_____

_____

_____ .

3

All About Me Spanish Write & Read Books • Scholastic Professional Books •

Te presento a mi familia

por _____

(Dibuja aquí a tu familia.)

Hay _____ personas en mi familia.

Se llaman _____

_____

_____

_____ .

Este es el dibujo del lugar dónde vive mi familia.

En mi casa, mi familia habla el idioma

_____ .

1

Estas son las cosas que en mi familia hacemos juntos.

(Encierra en un círculo lo que hacen juntos en tu familia.)

Jugar juegos.

Escuchar música.

Ir al parque.

Comer.

Leer libros.

Mirar la tele.

También nos gusta _____

_____

_____

_____.

2

○ Mi lugar favorito en mi casa es _____

_____ .

Este es el dibujo de mi lugar favorito en mi casa.

Me gusta este lugar porque _____

_____

_____

_____ .

3

Te presento a mi amigo/a,

_____

por _____

Este es el retrato de mi amigo/a.

Me gusta mi amigo/a porque _____

_____

_____

_____.

1

Estas son las cosas que me gusta hacer con mi amigo/a. (Encierra en un círculo las cosas que te gusta hacer con tu amigo/a.)

Jugar juegos.

Hacer rompecabezas.

Hacer deportes.

Jugar juegos en la computadora.

Jugar con muñecos.

Construir con bloques.

También nos gusta _____

_____

_____.

2

¡Es Halloween!

por _____

Para Halloween me disfrazaré de

_____.

En este dibujo estoy con mi disfraz de Halloween.

1

El año pasado me disfracé de

_____.

El año que viene quizás me disfrace así.

(Encierra en un círculo los disfraces que podrías elegir

para el año que viene.)

animal

fantasma

monstruo

superhéroe

bruja o mago

O quizás me disfrace de _____

_____.

2

Estas son las cosas que me gusta hacer en Halloween.

_____

_____

○ _____

_____

_____ .

Me gusta Halloween porque _____

_____

○ _____

_____

_____

_____ .

3

¡Feliz Día de Acción de Gracias!

por _____

En el Día de Acción de Gracias pensamos en todo por lo que damos gracias.

En este dibujo enseño las cosas por las que doy gracias.

Doy gracias por _____

porque _____

_____

_____ .

1

Esto es lo que me gusta comer en el Día de Acción de Gracias. (Encierra en un círculo los alimentos que te gusta comer en el Día de Acción de Gracias.)

pavo

jamón

verduras

relleno

pastel
de calabaza

pan

También me gusta comer _____

_____

_____

_____

_____.

2

All About Me Spanish Write & Read Books • Scholastic Professional Books •

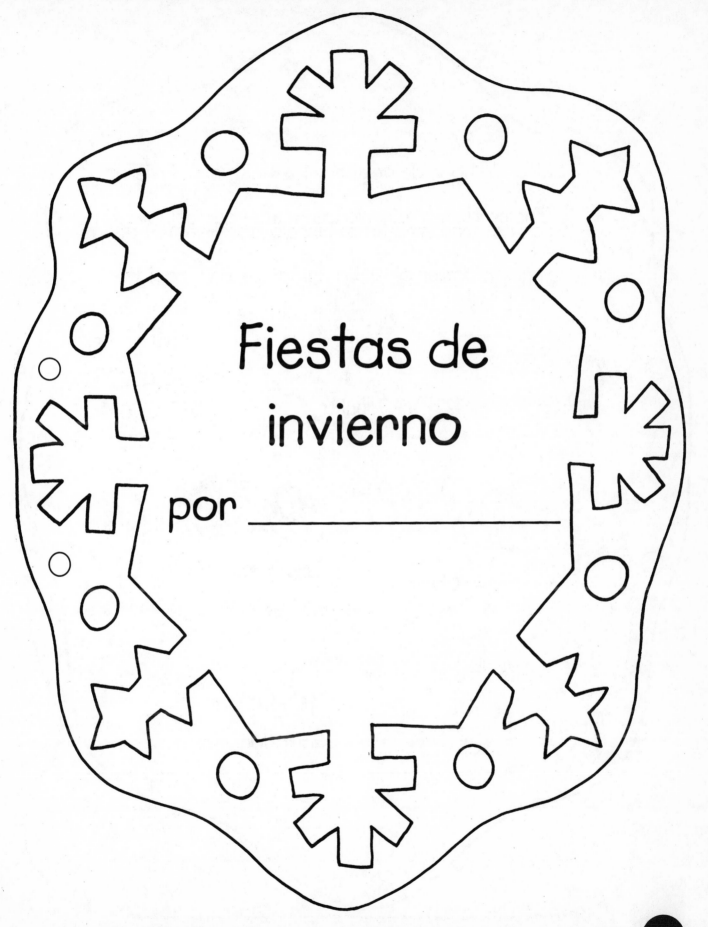

Fiestas de invierno

por _____

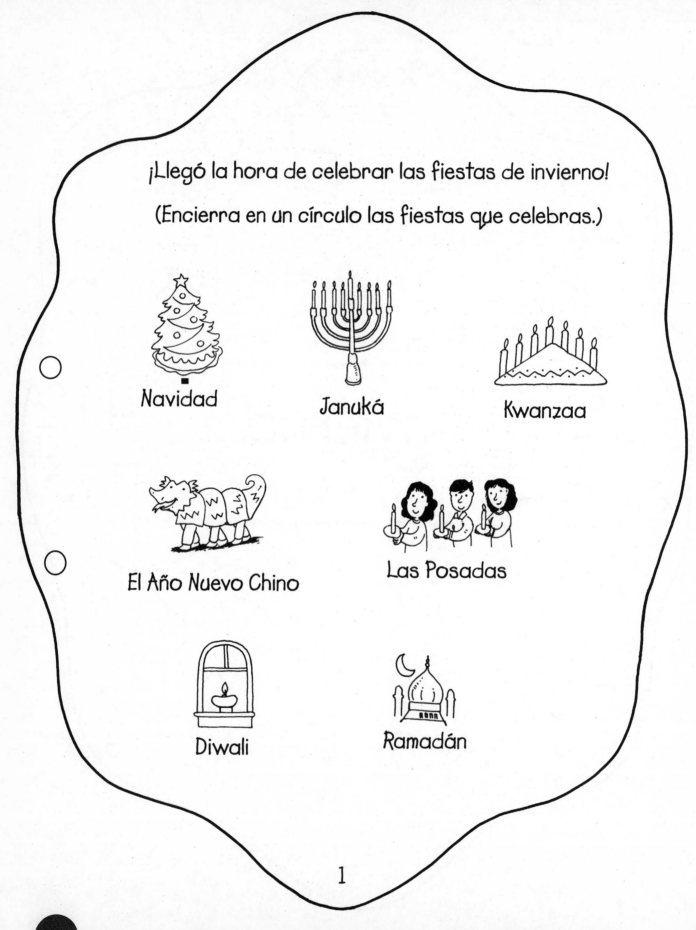

¡Llegó la hora de celebrar las fiestas de invierno!

(Encierra en un círculo las fiestas que celebras.)

Navidad

Januká

Kwanzaa

El Año Nuevo Chino

Las Posadas

Diwali

Ramadán

1

Yo celebro estas fiestas con otras personas. Ellos se llaman

_____

_____.

Este dibujo es de algo especial que hacemos en esas fiestas.

En este dibujo estoy _____

_____

_____.

2

Este es el dibujo de lo que me gusta comer en esta fiesta.

Mi comida favorita en esta fiesta es

_____

_____.

Las fiestas son especiales porque _____

_____

_____.

3

El libro de
mi cumpleaños

por _____

Tengo _____ años de edad.

Mi cumpleaños es el _____ de _____.
                        (día)   (mes)

Los cumpleaños son divertidos porque _____

_____

_____

_____

_____

1

Este es el dibujo de lo que me gustaría hacer en mi cumpleaños.

En mi cumpleaños, me gustaría _____

_____

_____.

Me gustaría celebrar mi cumpleaños con estas

personas: _____

_____.

2

Este es el dibujo de lo que me gustaría comer en mi cumpleaños.

En mi cumpleaños, también me gustaría comer

_____

_____

_____ .

3

All About Me Spanish Write & Read Books • Scholastic Professional Books •

¡Es hora de comer!

por _____

Estas son algunas de las comidas que me gusta comer.

(Encierra en un círculo lo que te gusta comer.)

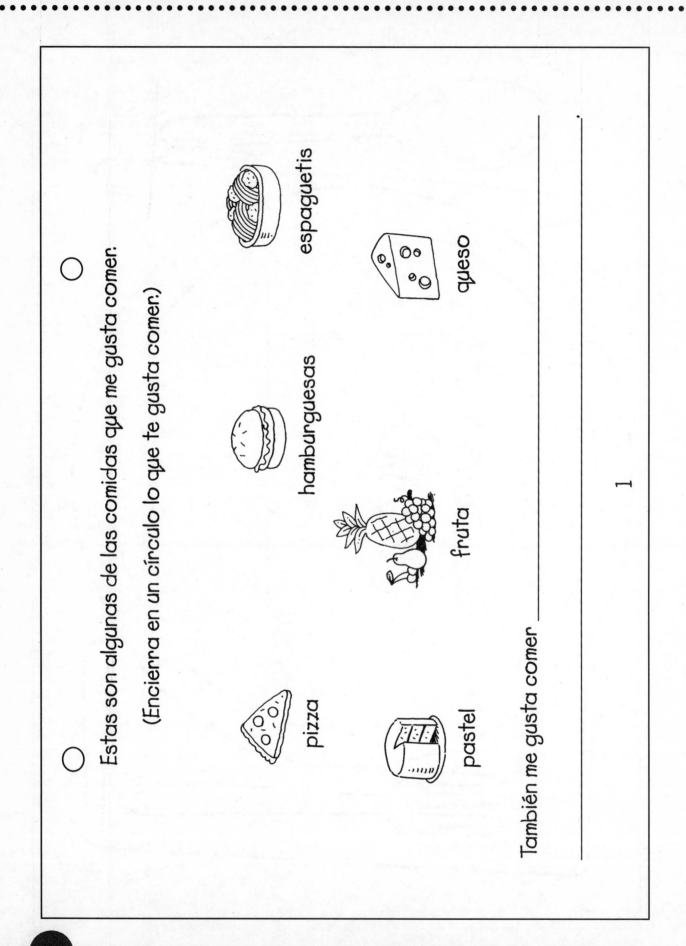

espaguetis

queso

hamburguesas

fruta

pizza

pastel

También me gusta comer

1

Para el desayuno me gusta comer _____.

Para el almuerzo me gusta comer_____.

2

En la cena me gusta comer _____.

Este es el dibujo del postre que me gusta.

3

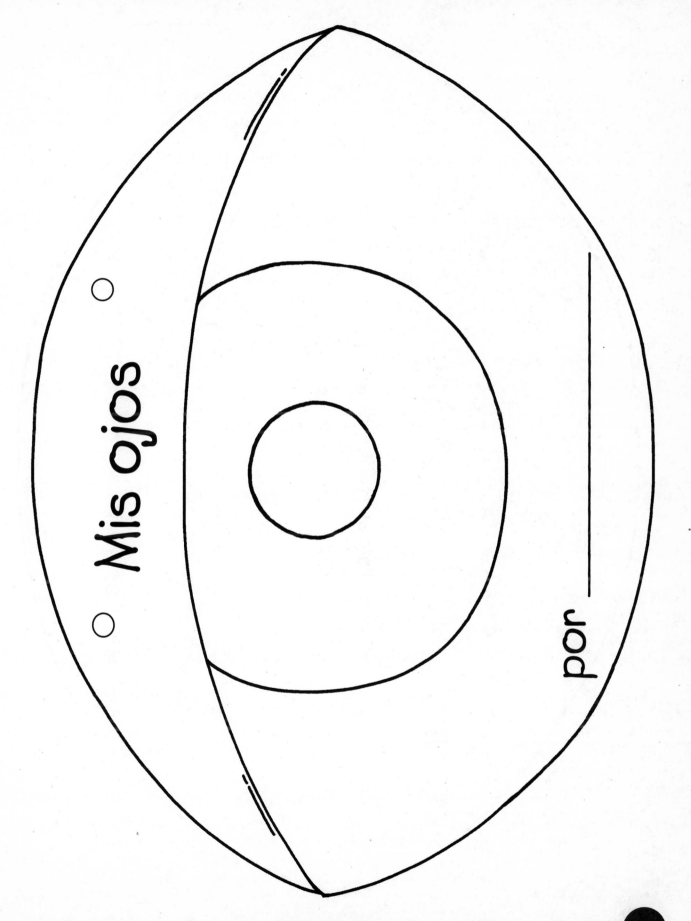

Mis ojos

por _____

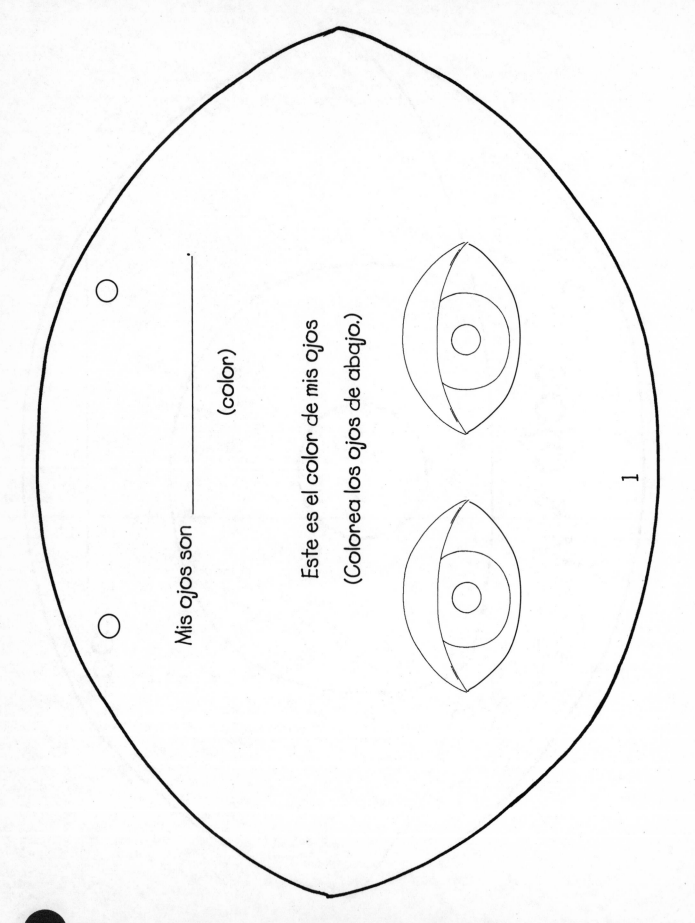

Mis ojos son _____

(color)

Este es el color de mis ojos

(Colorea los ojos de abajo.)

1

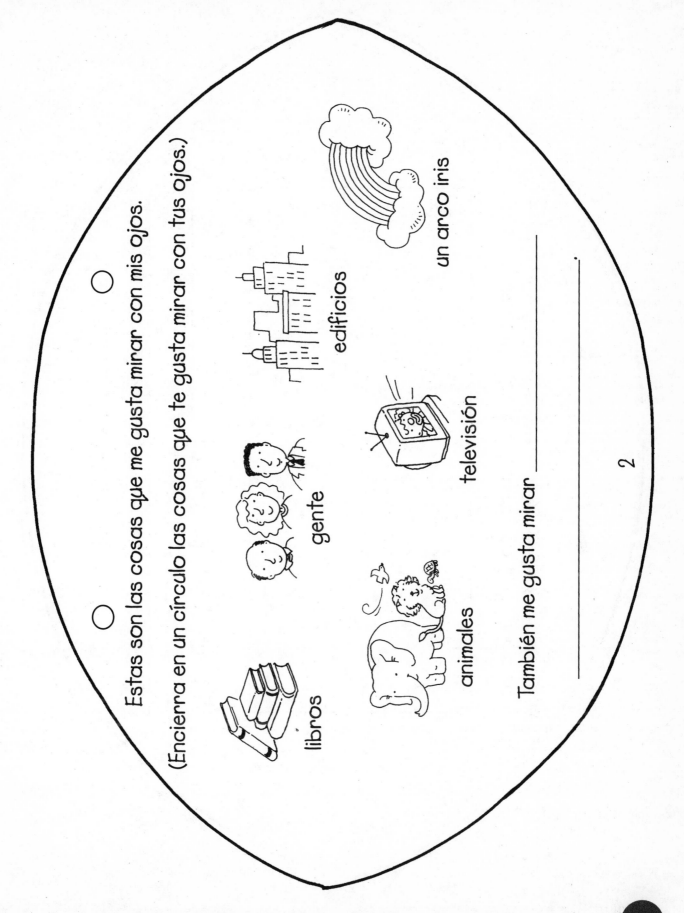

Estas son las cosas que me gusta mirar con mis ojos.

(Encierra en un círculo las cosas que te gusta mirar con tus ojos.)

un arco iris

edificios

gente

televisión

libros

animales

También me gusta mirar _____

2

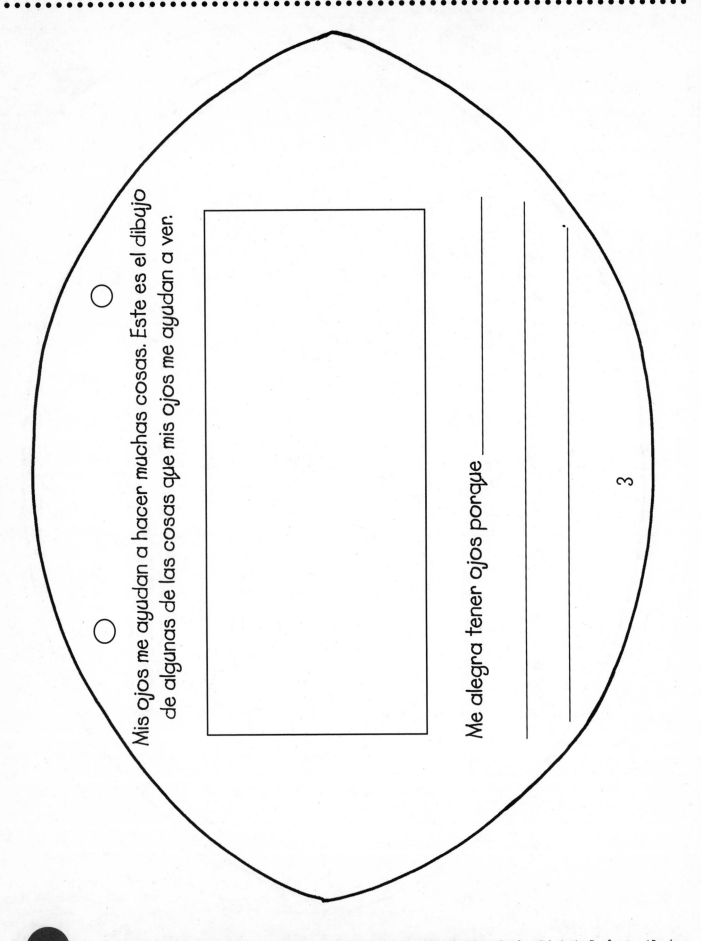

Mis ojos me ayudan a hacer muchas cosas. Este es el dibujo
de algunas de las cosas que mis ojos me ayudan a ver.

Me alegra tener ojos porque

3

Mi animal favorito

por _____

Este animal me gusta porque _____

_____

_____.

Este es el dibujo de mi animal favorito.

1

Mi animal favorito tiene estas cosas.

(Encierra en un círculo las cosas que tu animal

favorito tiene.)

○

pelaje

bigotes

plumas

aletas

escamas

garras

○

Mi animal favorito es más grande que _____

_____,

pero más pequeño que _____

_____.

2

Esto es algo que sé sobre mi animal favorito:

_____

_____

_____ .

Esto es algo que quiero saber sobre mi animal favorito:

_____

_____

_____ .

Si mi animal favorito fuera mi mascota, lo llamaría

_____ .

3

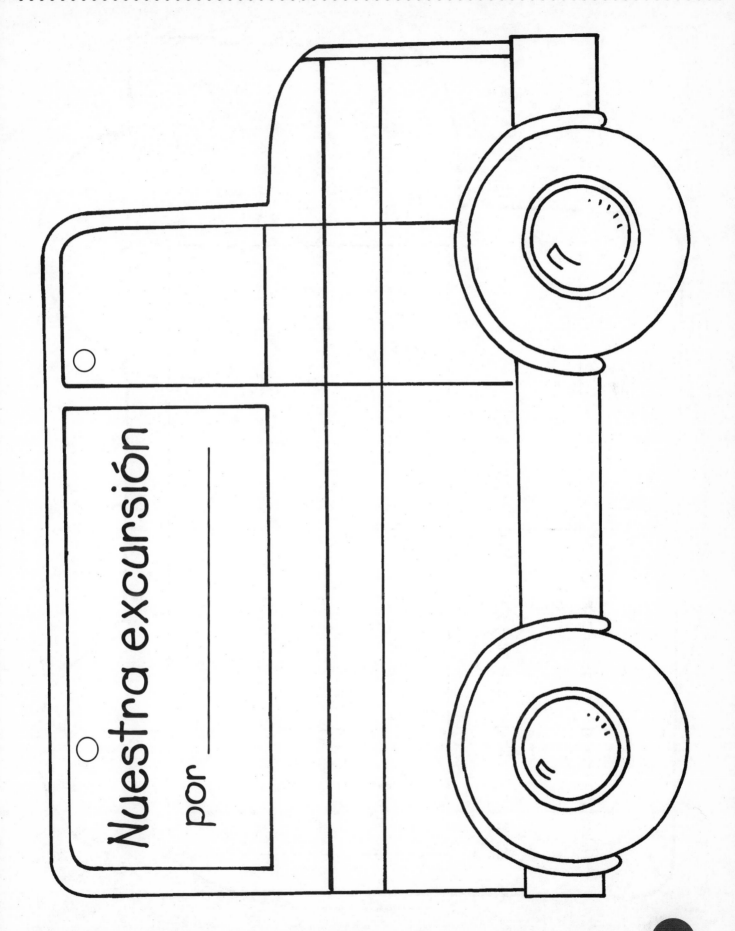

Nuestra excursión

por _____

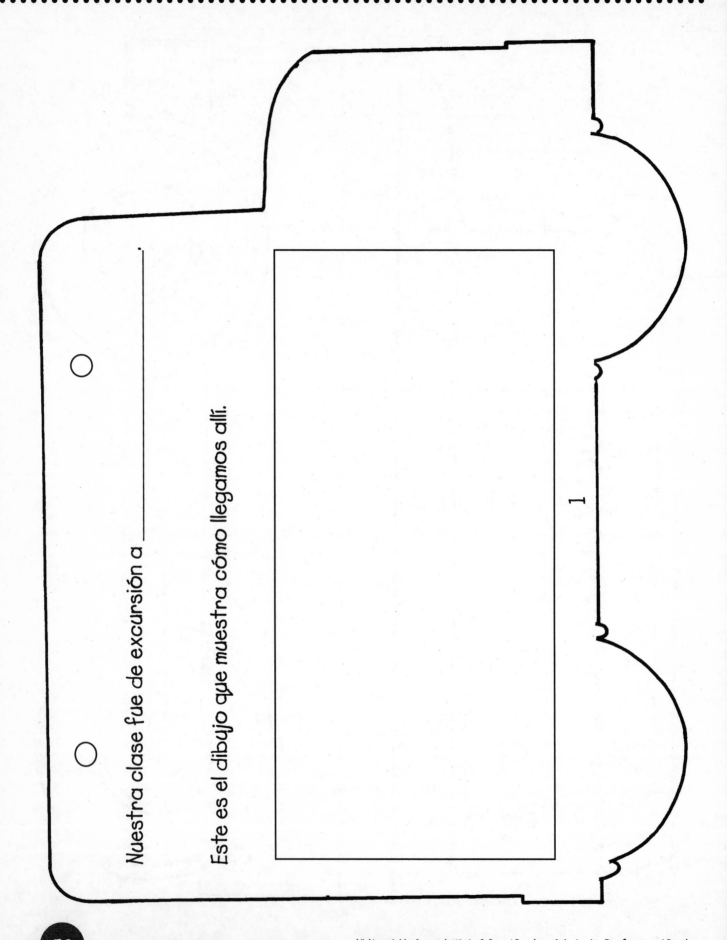

Nuestra clase fue de excursión a _____

Este es el dibujo que muestra cómo llegamos allí.

1

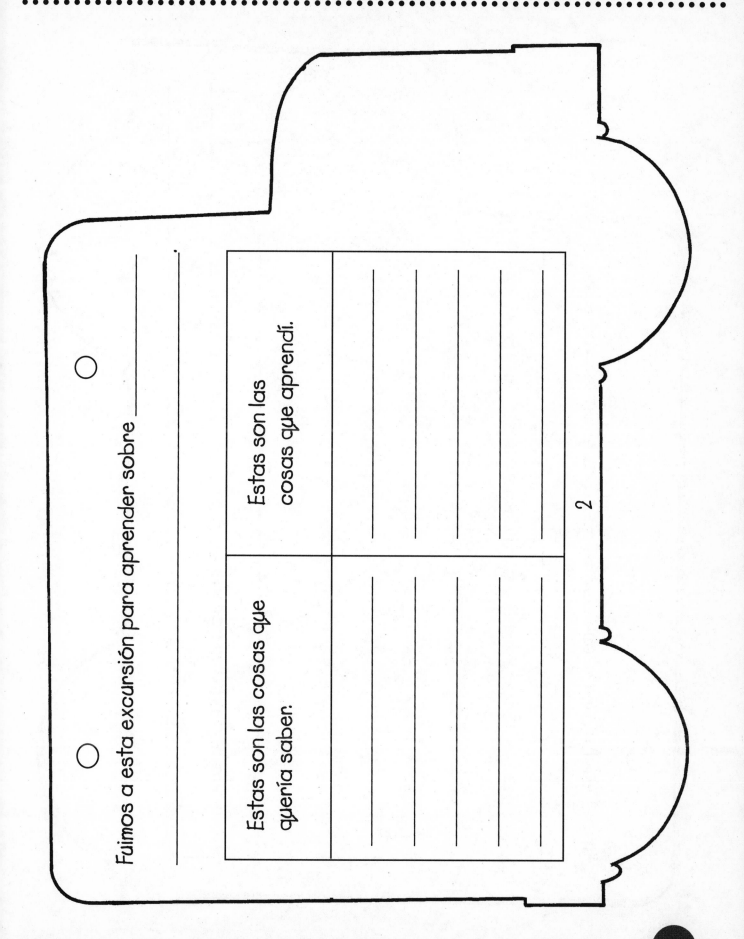

Fuimos a esta excursión para aprender sobre _____

Estas son las cosas que quería saber:

Estas son las cosas que aprendí.

2

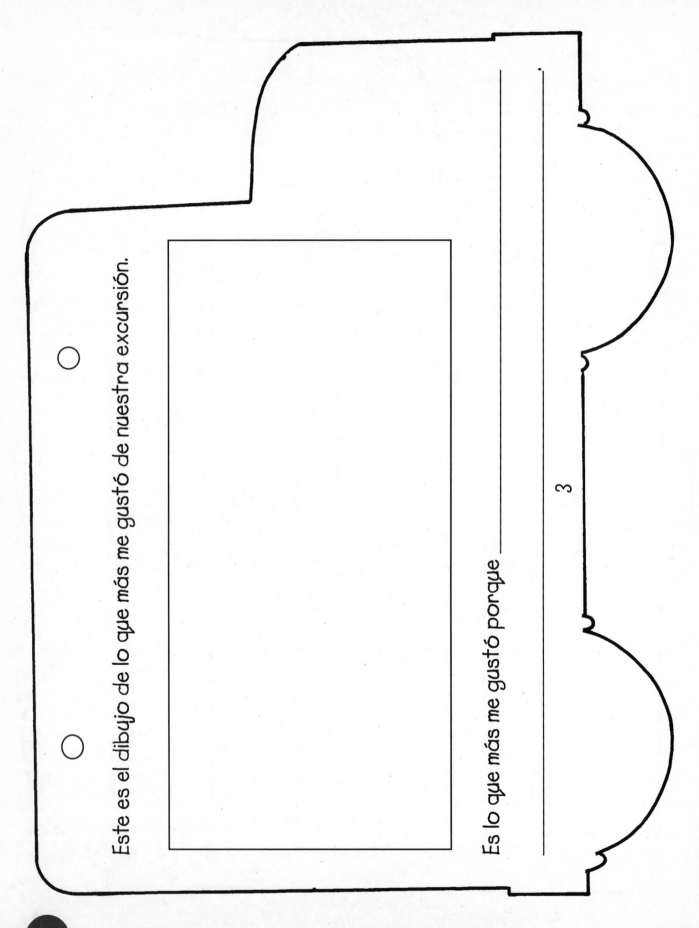

Este es el dibujo de lo que más me gustó de nuestra excursión.

Es lo que más me gustó porque _____

3

¿Qué tiempo hace?

por _____

Por mi ventana puedo ver que hoy el tiempo está así.

Hoy el tiempo está _____

1

Estas son las palabras que describen el tiempo en donde vivo.

(Encierra en un círculo las palabras que describen cómo es el tiempo en donde vives.)

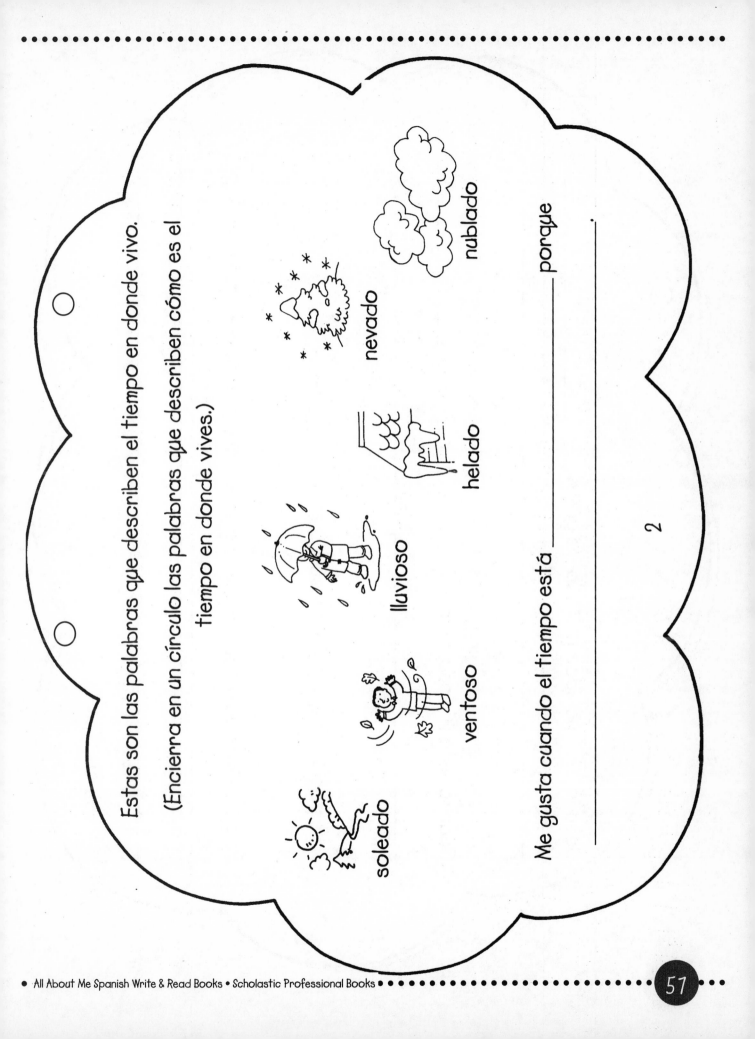

soleado

ventoso

lluvioso

helado

nevado

nublado

Me gusta cuando el tiempo está _____ porque _____

2

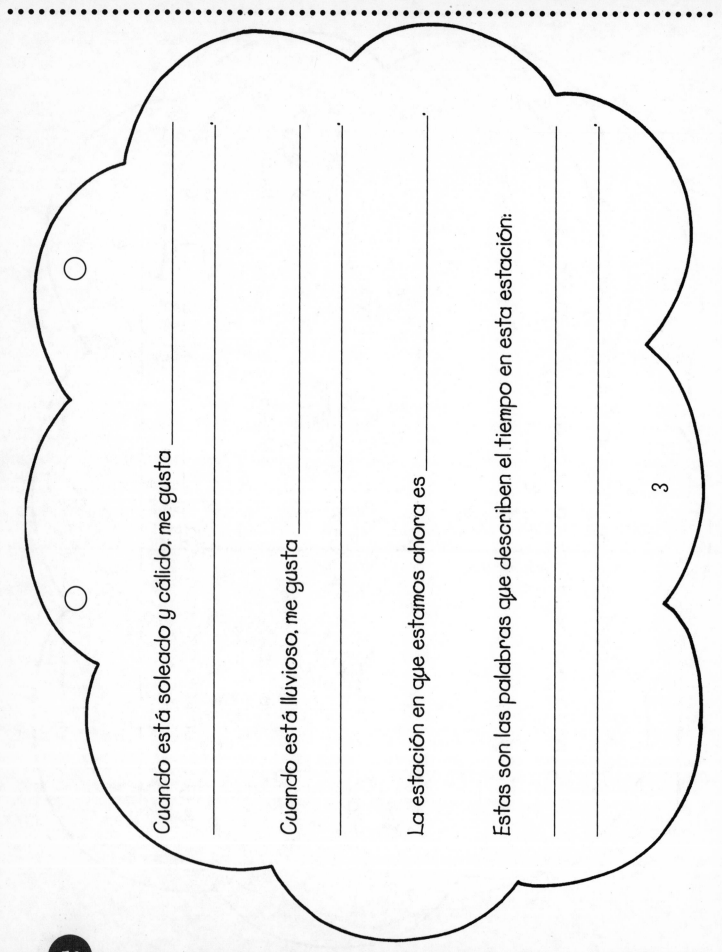

Cuando está soleado y cálido, me gusta _____

Cuando está lluvioso, me gusta _____

La estación en que estamos ahora es _____

Estas son las palabras que describen el tiempo en esta estación: _____

3

¡Vivan los libros!

por

_____

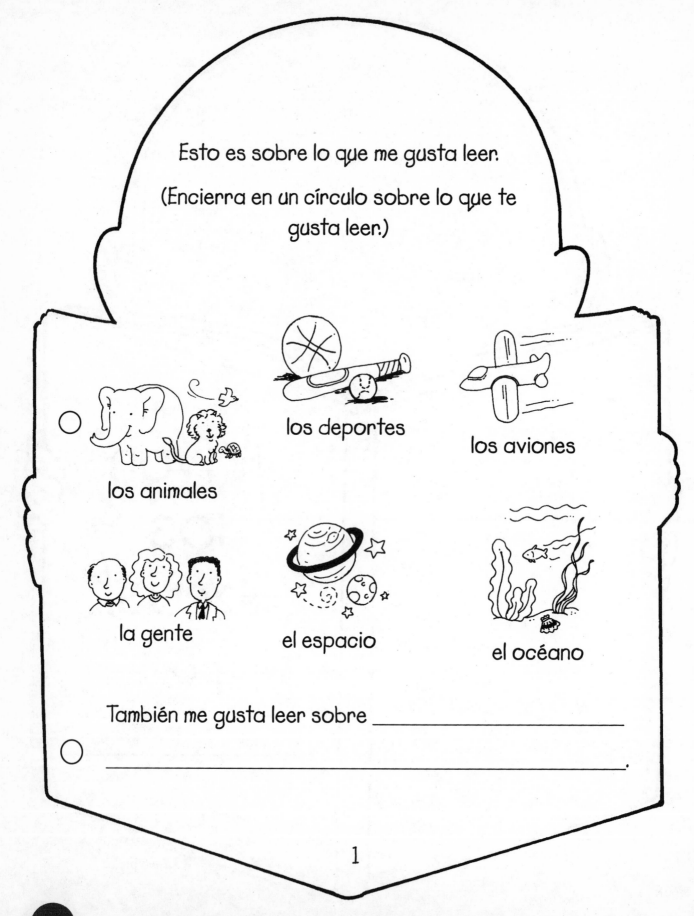

Esto es sobre lo que me gusta leer.

(Encierra en un círculo sobre lo que te gusta leer.)

los deportes

los aviones

los animales

la gente

el espacio

el océano

También me gusta leer sobre _____

_____.

1

Uno de mis libros favoritos es _____

_____.

La tapa del libro se parece a esta.

Este libro trata de _____

_____.

Me gusta este libro porque _____

_____.

2

Cuando sea grande...

por_____

All About Me Spanish Write & Read Books • Scholastic Professional Books

Esto es lo que quisiera ser cuando
sea grande.

(Encierra en un círculo uno o más.)

maestro/a

doctor/a

policía

artista

astronauta

atleta

O me gustaría ser _____

_____ cuando sea grande.

1

Este es mi retrato como

_____.

(lo que quisieras ser cuando seas grande.)

Me gustaría ser _____

porque _____

_____.

Es un trabajo importante porque _____

_____

_____.

2